THE VEGAN KETO DIET BOOK #2020

Vegan Weight Loss Recipes for Every Day incl. 28 Days Vegan Challenge

NICHOLAS CLARKE

TABLE OF CONTENTS

INTRODUCTION

It is a fact that healthy living improves the general quality of life. The most fundamental approach to healthy living starts right from your kitchen. While others may adopt an active lifestyle, it is indeed a secondary option after healthy eating. However, if you can be able to mix up the two, kudos, you are exactly where you should be. Keeping healthy and watching weight is often a task that is daunting to many. For this reason, we have a vegan Keto diet plan that is effortless and ensures a steady loss in weight; but more fundamentally enables you to live a healthy and long life.

THE KETO VEGAN DIET

To begin, a Keto diet is essentially a high fat, low carb, and an average protein diet known for its overall health benefits. While a Keto diet is hugely made up of animal products, this type of diet can also be utilized and incorporated by other diet plans for this case, the vegan diet. Typically, a vegan diet is a purely plant-based type of diet which ideally, reduces the numerous animal products meal options which makes it relatively difficult to maintain a low carb diet. Nonetheless, with careful planning and understanding of the right tweaks in your recipes, vegans can also equally reap the full benefit of the Ketogenic diet.

How does the Keto diet work?

The Keto diet is definitely taking the world by storm and you must have heard about the health benefits it comes with, but do you know how it works? To begin, the body naturally generates energy through the breaking down of glucose. This particular approach is the most convenient way the body can generate energy. While it is the most efficient route, the burning of carbs comes with one major setback. The fats that you take in with your meals largely remain unused and are stored in the body reservoir for a rainy day. As a consequence, over time you gain weight hence predisposing yourself to other health complications. The Keto diet limits the intake of carbs to the recommended 50g a day. This forces the body to initiate the Ketosis process. The Ketosis phase forces the body to switch to fat as the preferred source of getting energy to compensate for the shortage of carbs. The Ketosis phase produces Ketones that help breakdown fats in the liver. Therefore, while you will be enjoying your meals, you will also be burning fat at the same time making you lose weight in the long run.

The vegan Keto diet and muscle building.

The process of building muscle is one that is hugely misunderstood by many. The claims that you only require a high carb intake to build muscle will always remain a misconception. Going back to the basics, building muscle requires a proper training regiment, enough proteins, and a constant caloric surplus which can easily be achieved while on a vegan keto diet. However, let's face it, while on a high carb diet, you will indeed gain mass quickly only because you are also accumulating fat as well. The beauty of building muscle while on a Keto diet is that you will only build lean muscle hence giving you that diamond cut physique. Who doesn't want that! While it may take you some time, the overall result will be worth the wait.

Types of Keto diet and getting the right one for you

There are three main types of Keto diets. A proper understanding of these variations will make it easier for you to decide the right one for you. Let's get right in!

The standard Keto diet

This is the most basic of all Keto diet plan variations. It is quite easy and straight forward which makes it great for anyone who is considering getting into the diet plan. The only thing to always keep in mind is observing and sticking to healthy fatty meals.

Cyclic Ketogenic diet

This variation is usually recommended for bodybuilders who constantly require a high caloric surplus and constantly replenishing their glycogen stores. The CKD works by restricting you to the basic traditional Keto diet for 5 days a week and get off for 2 days. The off days give the individuals in this plan the flexibility of getting in more carbs to boost their glycogen levels which is fundamental for bodybuilding. However, be sure to only consume whole carbohydrates and legumes.

Targeted Ketogenic diet

This variation is for anyone who has an active lifestyle. Whether you go for morning runs or need that extra boost for your gym sessions, this specific variation is designed for just that. Under the targeted Keto diet, you have the flexibility of taking in 20-30 grams of carbs before and after your workout to give you that boost of energy before your workouts and hasten recovery thereafter.

How will your body react to the Keto diet?

Whether you are vegan or not, your body is used to the same old cycle of getting energy from carbohydrates. When you change things up from the blues, your body will definitely need some adapting to do. You should know that the first week will be the most difficult since your body is transitioning. You may feel slight headaches and dizziness as signs of electrolyte loss. This should not be a concern because constant hydration and taking in food rich in sodium will help replenish those lost electrolytes. In no time, your body will develop more fat-burning enzymes and adjust accordingly.

The Keto lifestyle and why it is good for you

The Keto diet is known for its immense health and wellness benefits making it one of the most sought after diets currently. Let's discuss some of the health benefits you should expect while on the diet.

Weight loss

The shift from getting your energy from carbs to fats does so much when it comes to weight loss. In fact, the Keto diet is the most comfortable diet that melts fat fast and at the same time requiring so little from you. While on the diet, you don't have to watch your meal portions or go into any form of fasting, making it very comfortable for you. Who said losing weight has to be painful!

Blood sugar control

Diabetes and weight issues often go hand in glove. While any other diet can help get your weight down, the Keto diet plan has proven to have so much good for diabetes type 2 patients. Studies have it that a Keto diet could help a type 2 diabetes patient get off drugs completely. This is because the Keto diet reduces the daily carb intake which the body benefits from since the blood sugar levels will remain low but within the healthy limit. The Keto diet will help keep your blood sugar levels within the normal range, therefore, keeping you at arm's length from getting type 2 diabetes.

Easy to maintain

The Keto diet will require very little from you making it effortless to maintain. However, we have to remain alive to the fact that the Vegan approach cuts down most of the necessary animal products for the Keto diet. However, knowing the right ingredients and spices can improve the taste and recipe, therefore, making the meals tastier.

Improved mental clarity and cognitive performance

There is no doubt that the Keto diet is good for your body; what is unknown to many is that the process is even beneficial to the brain. Here is why. As the brain cells age, they lose the ability to utilize glucose as the source of energy. Ketones, therefore, is a better alternative that will maintain the health of the aging brain cells. Through this, your brain will work efficiently and keep you sharp for longer.

Improved blood pressure

A normal blood pressure which is about 120mm/Hg according to an American Heart Association is usually an indication of a clean bill of health. When the pressure gets to 80-90mm Hg, this condition is described as hypertension. Hypertension is often associated with strokes, cardiac arrests among other fatal ailments. The Keto diet seems to combat high blood pressure more than any other diet out there. According to The Journal of American Medicine of 2017, a simple high fat low carb diet proved to be very effective in reducing hypertension. This was as a result of a significant increase in the amount of good cholesterol (HDL). So if you notice an increase in cholesterol levels while on this diet, it is usually a good thing.

WHAT TO EAT AND WHAT NOT TO EAT

Encouraged

Vegetables

Vegetables are an important part of both the Keto and vegan diet especially when the two diets are combined, you will be eating quite a lot of veggies in a day. A common misconception is that veggies are not the best-tasting meal in the world, but we are here to change that. Getting the right spices to go with your veggies will improve their taste and you will enjoy every single bite. Another tip that you should give it a try is topping your salads with a generous amount of olive oil. That rich taste will transform your meals making it enjoyable every time. Stay away from the vegetables that grow below ground because of their high carb content

Avocados

The avocado is a source of the necessary minerals like potassium that is absolutely beneficial to get you to that Ketosis phase. Avocadoes should be your ideal go-to Keto diet thanks to the low net carb content and high heart-healthy fat. With an average 4.5g of carb and almost 7g of fiber in a 3.5 ounce or 100g of serving, avocadoes are a great choice for any dietary habit.

Berries

Fruits are almost forbidden when on a Keto diet, however, you will be happy to know that most berries are not off-limits. Get ready to snack or spice your meals up with your favorite berries. However, as you enjoy your berry of choice, it is advised to watch on the amounts of blueberries you take, the carb content can easily add up.

Healthy oils

When you think of preparing meals the Keto way, olive and coconut oil are paramount. Olive oil exists in either the conventional one or the extra virgin version. The latter boasts of high oleic acid contents that are good for the heart while the latter has anti-inflammation properties and also boosts the artery function. Coconut oil has components that are easy for the liver to breakdown, absorb, and convert into Ketones. These two essential oils will help you lose weight and get rid of that gut.

Nuts

There are not so many snacks especially when on the vegan Keto diet making nuts a favorite go-to snack for many. In addition to giving you the essential fat necessary to get to the Ketosis stage, you should know that nuts are also rich in carbohydrates. It is better to incorporate them into your meals since you can actually account for the amounts you are taking rather than snacking on them. One general rule is to keep away from cashew nuts, you could easily pass your daily carb limit with only a few of those nuts.

Discouraged

Animal product meals

Animal products including milk, meat, and eggs are an important part of the Keto diet. However, this should be no excuse for not enjoying the full health benefits of the Keto diet if you are vegan. The plant-based diet comes with so many options that could easily replace the consumption of animal products, for example, the soy meat in place of animal meat and almond milk for regular milk from cows.

Starch

There are so many variations of starch that are a staple in so many countries. However, going Keto will need quite some sacrifice from you and that will mean staying away from the carbs completely. For the vegans, most of the carbs are plant-based and definitely reduces your options as far as meal options are concerned. One other source of starch that could easily be sneaked into your meals is legumes, while it is an important part of the vegan diet, they have a significantly high amount of carbohydrates therefore it is best to keep away from them. The silver lining in all these is that there are so many plant-based dietary options that you could replace this.

Fruits

Fruits are sweet, yes! But they contain a very high carb content that simply will not get you anywhere near that Ketosis phase. If you must indulge in this guilty pleasure, pick the smallest fruit of your choice and consume only one a week. Rather you could replace them with berries.

Alcohol

Alcohol is neither naturally vegan nor is it Keto friendly. This is because animal products could be used in making beer and also it essentially pure carbohydrates. Therefore, as a vegan who is on Keto keep clear of beer or any other alcohol for that matter.

Getting ready for my Keto Journey

Read books

You can never have too much knowledge, so get yourself a book that will open you up to the Keto and vegan diet. Getting a good book will let you in on good cooking techniques, different recipes, and also invaluable information on the diet. However, as you go out there and buy or rent a book make sure you get one from credible sources, for instance, doctors, dieticians, or scientists. A good recommendation is "Vegan Keto" by Liz Macdowen and "Vegan Keto diet for beginners" by Tyler Allen.

Clean up your refrigerator

Now that you have the knowledge in hand, it's time to give your refrigerator a complete upgrade. Go through the racks and trays removing everything that you will not be needing and only keeping the essentials. If you must keep some, only remain with a handful that you will finish before getting down with your diet. Remember if you keep what you don't need it is easy for you to fall for your cravings and get in the way of your Keto journey.

Stocking up

This is where all the fun begins if you love shopping as much as I do then you will enjoy this part. For now, you don't have to purchase everything at once, you will add more ingredients and supplies as you proceed further along with this journey. You could also buy additional ingredients as you learn new recipes. Stock up on the basics including vegetables, nuts, berries, essential oils, and some vegan-friendly spices. Avoid purchasing anything that is not good for the diet since you could easily fall for your cravings.

Eat before going out for shopping

This is a technique that is simple but very effective when you want to control impulse buying of the foods and snacks you don't need. It is good practice to have a small meal before going on grocery shopping. This will help keep your craving at bay and you will focus on exactly what you went there for.

Drink enough water

One common rule that applies whether you are on a diet or not is taking in enough water. The benefits of water in your body cannot be emphasized enough. While on the Keto diet, enough hydration is paramount especially in the first few days when the body is doing a lot of adjusting. If you do not know the amount of water you are supposed to take per day, get your body weight in pounds, and divide by two. Whatever you get, divide by eight, and that will be the amount of water your body requires per day. You could also decide to stick to the unspoken 8 glasses of water rule a day.

RECIPES

BREAKFAST

CARROT CAKE PANCAKES

Time: 30 minutes | Serves 3

Kcal 517, Carbs 5g/0.18oz., Fat44g/1.55oz., Protein 26g/0.88oz., Fiber 1g/0.03oz.

INGREDIENTS:

- Medium-sized grated carrot
- 68g/4 tablespoon dried coconut
- 30g/1 oz. of chopped walnuts
- 75g/2.5 oz. of raisins
- 4g/1 teaspoon of baking powder
- 34g/2 tablespoons arrowroot powder
- 180g/6.4 oz. plain flour
- 2g/½ teaspoon mixed spice powder
- 4g/1 teaspoon cinnamon powder
- 240 ml/2 cups of unsweetened dairy-free milk
- 10ml/2 teaspoons of apple cider vinegar
- 100g/3.5 oz. vegan cream cheese
- 5ml/1 teaspoon vanilla extract
- 60 ml/4 tablespoons coconut oil
- 120ml/8 tablespoons of maple syrup

PREPARATION:

1. Cook the grated carrots and walnuts in a nonstick skillet for a few minutes.
2. Begin by toasting the walnuts then removing from heat.
3. Put in the raisin and coconut then stir.
4. Mix the starch, flour, baking powder, and spices on a different bowl
5. Gently add in milk, oil, vinegar, and syrup and whisk till you achieve a fairly light consistent mixture.
6. Add in ¾ of the walnut and carrot mixture and stir. Remember to keep the mixture light.
7. Bring a dry pan to heat and add in ¼ a cup of the butter and cook one side before flipping to the other.
8. Repeat the same till you finish all the batter.
9. Combine the vegan cream cheese, vanilla extract, and syrup to achieve a smooth cream cheese frosting.
10. Serve 2 to 3 per plate and top with generous amounts of frosting and some carrot on the side.

CHEEZY CHORIZO & RED PEPPER FRITTATA

Time 40 minutes | Serves 2

Kcal 830, Carbs 9g/0.3oz.., Fats 77g/2.8oz.., Protein 42g/1.5oz.., Fiber 8g/0.25oz..

INGREDIENTS:

- 2 chorizo style vegan sausages
- 68g/4 tablespoons of grated mozzarella-styled vegan cheese
- 4ml/1 teaspoon of black salt
- 2ml/½ a teaspoon onion granule
- 14g/1 tablespoon coconut sugar
- 1 small chopped red pepper
- 15ml/ 1 tablespoon balsamic vinegar
- 75g/¾ a cup of chickpea flour
- A thinly sliced onion
- 15ml/1 tablespoon of olive oil
- 280g/10 oz. of drained fine tofu
- 180ml of water

- 2g/½ a teaspoon of ground black pepper

PREPARATION:

1. Bring the oven to 180°C/356°F
2. On a nonstick frying pan, sauté the onions for a few minutes using olive oil then add sugar and balsamic vinegar.
3. Fry for another five minutes till onions turn sticky before adding red pepper and further cook for 5 minutes.
4. Add everything except cheese to a food processor or hand mixer and blend to achieve an egg-like consistency.
5. Mix the egg-like mixture with the onion and pepper and stir till even.
6. Cut the vegan sausages into ½ inch slices and add to the frittata before sprinkling some cheese on top.
7. Bake in the oven for 20 minutes till the cheese melts and gets a golden brown color on top.
8. Serve while hot.

OVEN-BAKED RUTABAGA WEDGES

Time 20 minutes | Serves 4

Kcal 167, Carbs 7g/0.24oz., Fats 14g/0.5, Proteins 1g/0.03oz., Fibers 1g/0.01oz.

INGREDIENTS:

- 450g/1 lb. rutabaga
- 60ml/¼ cup olive oil
- Pepper and salt
- 4g/1 teaspoon chili powder

PREPARATION:

1. Allow the oven to heat to a temperature of 200°C/400°F.
2. Rinse before peeling the rutabaga.
3. Slice into wedges and spread evenly on the baking sheet
4. Add some pepper and salt before topping with some olive oil.
5. Bake in the oven for 20 minutes till the rutabaga wedges get that nice color.

VEGAN KEBAB ROLLS WITH GARLIC SAUCE

Time: 60 minutes | Serves 4

Kcal 1124, Carbs 16g/0.6oz., Fats 103g/3.6oz., Proteins 32g/1.13oz., Fiber 14g/0.5oz.

INGREDIENTS:

The vegan Kebab

- 🍴 64g/ ½ cup of sliced almond
- 🍴 230g/8oz. of sliced mushrooms
- 🍴 64g/ ½ cup of pumpkin seeds
- 🍴 125ml/½ cup if divided olive oil
- 🍴 68g/ 4 tablespoons of chia seeds
- 🍴 96g/¾ cup vegan unflavored protein powder
- 🍴 Single pressed garlic clove
- 🍴 34g/2 tablespoons of chopped fresh parsley

- 🍴 8g/ 2 teaspoons of cumin
- 🍴 8g/ 2 teaspoons of onion powder
- 🍴 4g/ 1 teaspoon of ground coriander seeds
- 🍴 1g/ ¼ teaspoon of ground black pepper
- 🍴 A pinch of salt
- 🍴 ¼ a cup of water

Garlic sauce

- 🍴 45ml/3 tablespoons of aquafaba
- 🍴 15ml/ 1 tablespoon lemon juice
- 🍴 A pinch of salt

- 🍴 8g/ 2 teaspoons dried mint
- 🍴 2 pressed cloves of garlic
- 🍴 250ml/1 cup of light olive oil

Vegetables

- 🍽 A red onion
- 🍽 2 tomatoes
- 🍽 1 Romaine lettuce
- 🍽 Small cucumber
- 🍽 64g/½ cup of chopped parsley

PREPARATION:

1. Bring the oven to 175°C/350°F.
2. On a large dry frying pan, fry the pumpkin and almond seeds till nice and fragrant before pulsing on a food processor for some minutes.
3. Using a third of the olive oil, fry the mushrooms till soft.
4. Put all the remainder of the Kebab ingredients, the mushrooms, and some oil in the food processor and mix.
5. Let the mixture sit for 5 minutes before shaping sausage-shaped kebabs out of the mixture.
6. Bake the sausage kababs in the oven till nice and brown.
7. As the kebab cooks, put garlic, lemon juice, and aquafaba in the blender and blend for 30 seconds.
8. Pour in olive oil slowly as you continue mixing at full speed to achieve a creamy paste.
9. Finish by mixing with mint and some salt.
10. Wash and separate the lettuce before mixing with chopped cucumber and some parsley.
11. On each serving, top the lettuce with a kabab, some garlic sauce, and salad on the side.

VEGAN TOFU SCRAMBLE

Time: 20 minutes | Serves 2

Kcal 281, Carbs 2g/0.07, Fats17g/0.6oz., Protein 35g/1.23oz., Fiber 1g/0.03oz.

INGREDIENTS:

- 370g/ 13 oz. of firm tofu
- 17g/1 tablespoon of nutritional yeast
- 1g/¼ a teaspoon of Turmeric
- Pepper and salt
- 180ml/¾ a cup of unsweetened almond milk
- 17g/1 tablespoon of chopped fresh chives

PREPARATION:

1. Break the tofu into fairly large pieces in a large nonstick pan. Not any smaller than a mouthful, they break further while cooking.
2. Put in some turmeric and nutritional yeast combine carefully before cooking for 5 minutes.
3. Pour in almond milk and simmer over medium heat for 10 minutes. Keep stirring occasionally till the softens into a creamy paste.
4. Add pepper and salt and top with some chives.

LOW CARB EGGPLANT TOWERS

Time: 40 minutes | Serves 4

Kcal 558, Carbs 9g/0.3oz., Fats 49g/1.7oz., Proteins 19g/0.7oz., Fiber 6g/0.2oz.

INGREDIENTS:

- 400g/14oz. fresh basil

- Ground black pepper

- A pinch of salt

- 1 clove of garlic

- 125ml/ ½ a cup of extra virgin oil

- 1 eggplant about 500g/17 oz.

- 30ml/2 tablespoons of olive oil

- 2 tomatoes

- 260g/ 9 oz. vegan mozzarella cheese

- 115g/4 oz. cherry tomatoes

PREPARATION:

1. Blend garlic, some salt, basil, and olive oil in a food processor till smooth for that delicious basil dressing.
2. Slice the mozzarella, tomatoes, and eggplant into 1cm/½ inch pieces.
3. Over medium heat, fry the eggplants in olive oil until nice and golden.
4. To make the tower, place a piece of eggplant at the center of the plate followed by mozzarella and tomato in that order.
5. Top with a generous drip of basil dressing over each tower.
6. Repeat that particular arrangement till all the ingredients are used, each tower should have 6 slices.
7. Finish with another topping of basil dressing and half slices of cherry tomatoes arranged beautifully around the plate.

LOW CARB VEGAN VANILLA PROTEIN SHAKE

Time: 10 minutes | Serves 1

Kcal 450, Carbs 3/0.1oz., Fats 24g/0.8oz., Proteins 12g/0.4oz., fiber 9g/0.3oz.

INGREDIENTS:

- 125ml/½ cup unsweetened almond milk
- 125ml/½ cup of coconut milk
- 25g/1 oz. of frozen cauliflower rice
- 17g/ 1 tablespoon almond butter
- 68g/4 teaspoon of unflavored protein powder
- 5ml/ 1 teaspoon vanilla extract
- 2g/½ teaspoon ground cinnamon

PREPARATION:

1. Combine all the ingredients and pour them into a blender.
2. Blend continuously at full speed until you achieve a smooth mixture.
3. Pour in your favorite glass and put in two ice cubes and enjoy it cold!

LUNCH

AVOCADO AND RADISH SALAD AND FENNEL CARROT

Time: 45 minutes | Serves 2

Kcal 554, Carbs 14g/0.49oz., Fats 43g/1.5oz., Proteins 15g/0.16oz., Fiber 9g/0.3oz.

INGREDIENTS:

- 56g/ 2oz. Sesame seeds

- 2 carrots

- 75ml/5 tablespoons tamari soy sauce

- 170g/6 oz. radishes

- An avocado

- 1 bulb fennel

- 30ml/2 tablespoon olive oil

- 56g/2 oz. leafy greens

- Ground black pepper

PREPARATION:

1. Bring the oven to 180°C/350°F and place a baking sheet and parchment paper.
2. Put the sesame seeds in a dish and pour in the soy sauce. Let the sesame seeds absorb the sauce for about 15 minutes, or until most of the sauce is absorbed.
3. Spread the sesame seed on the baking sheet and let it cook for 10 minutes until dry and crispy.
4. Peel and chop the radishes, carrots, and fennel into small pieces either by hand or with a mandolin.
5. Peel and slice the avocado into small pieces
6. Mix up the avocado, vegetables, leafy greens, and proper amounts of olive oil. Add some pepper and salt to your liking.
7. Finally, top with the baked sesame seeds and enjoy.

KETO FALAFELS

Time: 45 minutes | Serves 2

Kcal 577, Carbs 9g/0.32oz.., Fats 48g/1.7oz.., Proteins 28g/0.99oz., Fiber 6g/0.21g

INGREDIENTS:

- 60ml/¼ cup of water
- 4g/1 teaspoon ground coriander seeds
- 230g/8 oz. of sliced mushroom
- 125ml/½ cup of divided olive oil
- 64g/½ cup of pumpkin seed
- 4g/1 teaspoon onion powder.
- ½ cup of almonds
- 96g/¾ cup of vegan unflavored protein
- 2 cloves of garlic (minced)
- 34g/2 tablespoons of chopped parsley
- 4g/1 teaspoon salt
- 4g/1 teaspoon ground cumin
- 1g/¼ teaspoon of ground black pepper
- 68g/4 tablespoons of chia seeds

PREPARATION:

1. Bring the oven to a temperature of 175°C/350°F.
2. Roast the pumpkin seeds and almonds in a large frying pan till they are nice and fragrant.
3. Pulse the cooked pumpkin seeds on a food processor shortly
4. Using ⅓ of the olive oil, fry the mushrooms till soft and moist.
5. Pulse the combination of the remaining ingredients, mushrooms, and oil in the food processor for 4 minutes.
6. Set it aside and allow to rest for approximately 5 minutes.
7. After settling, roll the mixture into 1½ inch/4cm balls and place in baking sheets in preparation for baking.
8. Let the rolls bake for 20 minutes and serve when warm.

VEGAN TEMPEH PUMPKIN BOWL WITH HERB DRESSING

Time: 75 minutes | Serves 4

Kcal 859, Carbs 16g/0.6oz., Fats 82g/2.9oz., Proteins 23g/0.8oz., Fiber 2g/0.07oz.

INGREDIENTS:

Pumpkin

- 🍽 A pinch of salt
- 🍽 30ml/2 tablespoon olive oil
- 🍽 4g/1 teaspoon of smoked paprika powder
- 🍽 480g/17 oz. of pumpkins

Tempeh

- 🍽 1 clove of minced garlic
- 🍽 30ml/2 tablespoon olive oil
- 🍽 340g/12 oz. of long and narrow tempeh strips
- 🍽 4g/1 teaspoon of chili flakes
- 🍽 1g/¼ teaspoon of black pepper
- 🍽 30ml/ 2 tablespoons of tamari sauce

Herb dressing

- 🍽 250ml/1 cup of light olive oil
- 🍽 60ml/4 tablespoons of aquafaba
- 🍽 One minced garlic clove
- 🍽 5ml/1 teaspoon of lemon juice
- 🍽 A pinch of salt
- 🍽 68g/ 4 tablespoons of chopped parsley

Salad

- 🍽 50g/1¾ of baby spinach
- 🍽 50g/1¾ of arugula lettuce
- 🍽 32g/¼ a cup of toasted pumpkin seeds

PREPARATION:

1. To prepare the pumpkin, first, let the oven heat up to 175°C/350°F then line the baking tray with parchment paper.
2. Remove the seeds and slice the pumpkin into small manageable wedges
3. Put on the tray and add some olive oil before topping with some paprika powder and a pinch of salt.
4. Bake for 40-50 minutes until nice and tender.
5. While the pumpkin is baking, prep the tempeh by slicing into long narrow strips.
6. Mix the rest of the tempeh making ingredients in a bowl.
7. Put in the tempeh and let it marinate for about 10 minutes.
8. Now, fry the marinade together with the tempeh till you achieve nice brown color.
9. Put the aquafaba, lemon juice, garlic, and half of the parsley in a raised blender beaker.
10. Mix to achieve a frothy liquid before slowly adding in olive oil while running the blender.
11. Put in the other half of the parsley and stir through.
12. Serve the arugula and baby spinach together in a bowl. On an extra serving plate, put the leaves and top with the baked pumpkin, toasted pumpkin seeds, and some tempeh.

VEGAN BUDDHA BOWL

Time: 75 minutes | Serves 4

Kcal 466, Carbs 9g/0.32oz., Fats 31g/1.09oz., Protein 41g/1.44oz., Fiber 9g/0.32oz.

INGREDIENTS:

Spicy marinated tofu

- 8g/2 teaspoon of garlic ginger paste
- 8ml/1½ of sesame oil
- 6g/1½ of tamari soy sauce
- 2g/½ teaspoon of cayenne pepper
- 400g/14 oz. of cubed firm tofu

Buddha bowl

- Pepper and salt
- 15ml/1 tablespoon coconut oil
- 17g/1 tablespoon sesame seeds
- 140g/5 oz. of baby bok choy
- 140g/5 oz. of cauliflower florets
- 115g/4 oz. broccoli florets
- 70g/2½ oz. of sliced mushrooms
- 8g/½ a tablespoon of chopped parsley

PREPARATION:

1. Prepare the spicy tofu by putting all marinade ingredients and tofu cubes in a bowl before mixing and making sure the tofu is coated.
2. Place the mixture in the refrigerator and let the taste develop overnight.
3. Let the oven heat up to 175°C/350°F and line the baking tray with parchment paper.
4. Spread the tofu in one layer before baking to ensure even cooking.
5. Let the tofu cook in the oven for 35 minutes and remember to turn halfway through.
6. While the tofu is cooking, bring half of the coconut oil to heat on a frying pan.
7. Put in mushrooms and fry till you achieve a nice crisp finish and put away.
8. Use the food processer to blitz the cauliflower to small rice-like pieces.
9. Release the remainder of the coconut oil on a skillet and cook parsley and cauliflower rice for 5 minutes.
10. Microwave the broccoli on with some water until tender.
11. Half the baby bok choy. Splash some water onto a skillet, lay the baby bok choy cut phase down, and cook for 3 minutes over low to medium heat till tender.
12. To serve, place the cauliflower rice on one side of the plate, cooked baby bok choy on the other.
13. Finish on top with some fried mushroom and marinated tofu.
14. You could have some chili and sesame on the side if you so wish.
15. Add pepper and salt to your liking.

VEGAN KALE AND SPINACH SOUP

Time: 15 minutes | Serves 4

Kcal 914, Carbs 14g/0.49oz., Protein 11g/0.39oz.,
Fats 95g/3.35oz., fiber 11g/0.39oz.

INGREDIENTS:

- 230g/8 oz. kale
- 125ml/½ cup of coconut oil
- 230g/8 oz. fresh spinach
- 875ml/3½ cups of coconut milk
- 2 avocados

- 250ml/1 cup of water
- Pinch of salt
- 1 lime
- 1g/¼ teaspoon of ground black pepper

Fried kale

- Pepper and salt
- 2 chopped garlic cloves
- 10ml/2 teaspoons coconut oil
- 85g/2 oz. kale
- 1g/½ tsp of ground cardamom

PREPARATION:

1. Bring the coconut oil to heat on a pan.
2. Briefly, sauté the kales and spinach till they shrink and brown around the edges.
3. Put some water, avocado, and some spices before blending till creamy.
4. You can ask some lime juice at your own discretion.
5. Finally, fry garlic and kale preferably in high heat
6. Garnish soup before serving.

ZUCCHINI AND WALNUT SALAD

Time: 20 | Serves 2

Kcal 595, Carbs 8g/0.28oz., Fats 58g/2.05, Protein 9g/0.32oz., Fiber 7g/0.24oz.

INGREDIENTS:

- 32g/¼ cup of freshly cut chives

- 15ml/1 tablespoon of olive oil

- 2 zucchini

- 1 finely minced clove of garlic

- 10ml/2 teaspoons lemon juice

- 190ml/¾ cup of vegan mayonnaise

- 30ml/2 tablespoons of olive oil

- 2g/½ teaspoon of salt

- 1g/¼ teaspoon of chili powder

- One head of romaine lettuce

- 100g/3½ of chopped walnuts

- 115g/4 oz. of arugula lettuce

- Pepper and salt

PREPARATION:

1. Combine and whisk all the ingredients for making the dressing. Once mixed thoroughly, set aside to develop and blend flavors.
2. Put the romaine lettuce, chives, and arugula in a single bowl.
3. Cut and split the zucchini along the length then remove the seeds. Further cut the zucchini across into half-inch slices.
4. On a pan, bring olive oil to heat before adding the chopped zucchini. Add some pepper and a pinch of salt to your liking.
5. Sauté till you achieve a light brown color.
6. Combine the salad and zucchini before mixing thoroughly
7. Roast nuts in the same pan. Add some pepper and salt to taste.
8. Serve the nuts on the salad and top with the salad dressing.

VEGAN BUTTER CHICKEN

Time 30 minutes | Serves 4

Kcal 472, carbs 19g/0.67oz., Fats 32g/1.13oz., Protein 7g/0.25oz., Fiber0g

INGREDIENTS:

- 2g/½ teaspoon of garam masala
- 1g/¼ teaspoon chili powder
- 15ml/3 teaspoons of coconut oil
- 30ml/3 tablespoons of coconut milk
- A small onion
- A pinch of sea salt
- 2g/½ teaspoon of chili powder
- 1g/¼ teaspoon of ground ginger
- Medium head cauliflower
- 22ml/1½ tablespoon of coconut oil
- Juice of 1 lime
- 400g/14 oz. of coconut milk
- 2g/½ a teaspoon of ground black pepper

- 17g/1 tablespoon of garam masala
- 17g/1 teaspoon of curry powder
- 170g/6 oz. can of tomato paste
- 1g/¼ teaspoon of curry powder

PREPARATION:

1. Reduce the cauliflower into florets before combining with all the ingredients except oil in a large bowl.

2. Combine and stir carefully until every piece is coated with the marinade.

3. Put aside to marinate further.

4. Using a nonstick frying pan, bring the oil to heat up under high heat and char the marinated cauliflower florets until nice and brown.

5. Heat the remainder of the coconut oil and sauté the onions for 5 minutes until translucent.

6. Put in the seasons including sea salt, garam masala, chili powder, curry powder, and ground black pepper. Cook for 30 seconds.

7. Once is done, add in tomato sauce and coconut milk and mix everything up for 15 seconds.

8. Allow the mixture to boil shortly then reduce the heat and allow it to simmer for 5 minutes till nice and thick.

9. Pour in the cauliflower, toss, and stir till the cauliflower is coated evenly.

10. Reduce the heat and let the cauliflower cook and absorb up all the taste and flavors.

11. Add in some lime juice and blend well.

12. Remove from heat and garnish with some parsley and add salt to taste.

DINNER

PESTO ZUCCHINI NOODLES WITH CHERRY TOMATOES

Time: 25 minutes | Serves 2

Kcal 228, Carbs 7g/0.25oz., Proteins 4.5g/0.16oz.,
Fats 21g/0.74oz., Fiber 3.1g/0.11oz.

INGREDIENTS:

- 68g/4 tablespoons of low carb vegan pestos
- 2g/½ a teaspoon of ground black pepper
- 2g/½ a teaspoon of ground sea salt
- 64g/½ a cup of small cherry tomatoes
- 15ml/1 tablespoon of coconut oil
- 2 large zucchinis
- Vegan parmesan cheese

PREPARATION:

1. Roll the zucchinis into spirals and wrap-around with paper towels. Gently tap to absorb extra moisture from the noodles.
2. Over medium heat bring 12ml/¾ tablespoon of coconut oil to heat
3. Cook the zucchini noodles preferably for a minute until tender.
4. Cook the tomatoes on medium heat for 2 minutes till they burst slightly before removing from the heat.
5. Put in some pestos to your liking and toss to mix evenly. Add in the tomatoes and mix.
6. Serve with some sprinkle of the parmesan cheese on top.

VEGAN CAULIFLOWER PIZZA BITES

Time: 30 minutes | Serves 1

Kcal 72, Carbs 5.7g/0.2oz., Fats 7g/0.25oz., Proteins 2g/0.07, Fiber 3.7g/0.13oz.

INGREDIENTS:

- 🍽 An avocado

- 🍽 850g/30 oz. head of cauliflower

- 🍽 A flax egg

- 🍽 A pinch of salt

- 🍽 2g/½ teaspoon of ground pepper

- 🍽 2g/½ teaspoon of garlic powder

- 🍽 51g/3 tablespoons of marinara sauce

- 🍽 15ml/3 teaspoons of Italian seasoning

- 🍽 125g/½ cup of vegan shredded cheese

- 🍽 34g/2 tablespoons of vegan cheese

- 🍽 1g/¼ teaspoon of shredded red pepper flakes

PREPARATION:

1. Bring the oven to a temperature of 205° C/400° F then lay the muffin cup baking tray with a parchment paper.
2. Clean and shred the cauliflower into cauliflower rice using a mandolin.
3. In a microwave, cook the cauliflower rice on a bowl covered with a paper towel.
4. Allow the cauliflower rice to cool before bundling in a thin kitchen towel and squeeze out all the water.
5. Combine and mix the dry cauliflower rice with all the other ingredients except the avocado and cheese.
6. Scoop a tablespoon of the mix and distribute it equally in all the muffin cups. Remember to press tightly.
7. Bake for 15 minutes before adding the remaining cheese on top and heat for another 1 minute before removing from the oven.
8. Allow cooling for 15 minutes before removing from the pan.
9. Serve with some marinara sauce and mashed avocado seasoned with some pepper and salt on the side.

INSTANT POT PILAF

Time: 14 minutes | Serves 6

Kcal 100, Carbs 3.2g/0.11oz., Fats 7.2g/0.25oz., Protein 3.9g/0.13oz., Fiber 4.1g/0.14oz.

INGREDIENTS:

- 4g/1 teaspoon garlic powder
- 680g/24oz. of cauliflower
- 4g/1 teaspoon salt
- 60g/2 oz. of sunflower seeds
- 120ml/½ a cup of vegetable broth
- 17g/1 tablespoon of dried parsley
- Fresh parsley for garnish
- 15ml/1 tablespoon olive oil

PREPARATION:

1. Clean and cut the cauliflower using a grater into small rice-sized pieces.
2. Microwave the cauliflower in a bowl for 3 minutes.
3. Put the rice in a light kitchen cloth and squeeze to drain all the water.
4. In an instant pot, combine all the ingredients except the fresh parsley.
5. Be sure to break up the chunks of cauliflower rice that tend to clump up together.
6. Tightly secure the lid and let it cook for 4 minutes under pressure.
7. Allow the pot to settle for another 5 minutes before releasing the pressure.
8. Fluff the rice and serve with some fresh parsley garnish.

AIR FRYER CRISPY TOFU

Time: 40 minutes | Serves 4

Kcal 116, Carbs 2.7g/0.1oz., Fats 7.1g/0.25oz., Proteins 9.7g0.3oz., Fiber 1.6g/0.06oz.

INGREDIENTS:

- 🍽 4g/1 teaspoon of garlic powder

- 🍽 4g/1 teaspoon of paprika p

- 🍽 Pinch of sea salt

- 🍽 8g/2 teaspoons of cornstarch

- 🍽 3ml/½ teaspoon of liquid amino

- 🍽 3ml/½ teaspoon of sesame
  seeds oil

- 🍽 1g/¼ teaspoon of ground black
  pepper

- 🍽 2g/½ teaspoon of onion powder

- 🍽 450g/16oz. block of firm tofu.

PREPARATION:

1. Carefully cut the tofu block into 2½ cm/1inch cubes.
2. Put the tofu cubes in a bowl then add the liquid amino and toss around to coat each cube evenly.
3. Put in all the seasoning ingredients and toss around some more making sure the tofu cubes are well coated.
4. In the air fryer, arrange the tofu in a single row making sure each cube has space.
5. Cook the tofu in the air fryer under 205° C/400° F for 10 minutes. Remember to shake the basket halfway through.
6. Remove when the tofu is nice and brown an indication that it is cooked.
7. Let the tofu cool and enjoy!

THE KETO VEGAN KATHMANDU CURRY

Time:30 minutes | Serves 4

Kcal 401, Carbs 6.1g/0.22oz., Fats 14g/0.5oz., Protein12g/0.42oz., Fiber 4.9g/0.72oz.

INGREDIENTS:

- 400ml/3.5oz. full fat coconut milk
- 90g/¾ cup of raw pepitas
- 50g/2 ounces of cubed carrot
- 200g/2 cups of cubed zucchini

- 340g/3 cups of cauliflower rice
- 60g/½ a cup of raw sunflower seeds
- 90g/¾ cup of hulled hemp seed

Spices

- 4g/1 teaspoon of ground cumin
- 4g/1 teaspoon of ground coriander
- 2g/½ a teaspoon of ground Turmeric
- 2g/½ a teaspoon of ground ginger
- 2g/½ a teaspoon of granulated garlic
- A pinch of salt

- 2 bay leaves
- 1g/¼ a teaspoon of onion powder
- 1g/¼ a teaspoon of ground pepper
- 17g/1 tablespoon of madras curry powder

PREPARATION:

1. Clean and cut the cauliflower using a grater into small rice-sized pieces.
2. Microwave the cauliflower in a bowl for 3 minutes.
3. Put the rice in a light kitchen cloth and squeeze to drain all the water.
4. Place a pot on the burner and turn the heat on medium to light.
5. Put in all the ingredients and stir thoroughly till everything mixes up nicely.
6. Let the mixture cook for 25-30 minutes while the lid of the pot is covered.
7. Remember to stir constantly every 5 minutes until the carrots, zucchini, and the seeds have softened and the cauliflower rice is cooked.
8. Serve while warm.

PEANUT RED CURRY NOODLE BOWL

Time: 15 minutes | Serves 1

Kcal 355, Carbs 10.4g/0.37oz., Fats 23.4g/0.83oz., Proteins 16.8g/0.59oz., Fiber 16.9g/0.6oz.

INGREDIENTS:

- 225g/8 oz. shirataki noodles
- 10ml/2 teaspoons of Thai red curry
- 34g/2 tablespoons of unsweetened peanut butter
- 4g/2 teaspoons of low sodium tamari
- 1g/¼ a teaspoon of grated ginger
- 5ml/1 teaspoon of sesame oil
- 20g/¼ a cup of sliced bell peppers
- 5ml/1 teaspoon of fresh lime juice
- 45g/1.5 oz. of fresh edamame
- A pinch of red pepper flakes

PREPARATION:

1. Clean, drain and rinse the noodles carefully.
2. On low to medium heat, fry the noodle on a pan for a few minutes until they get dry.
3. Put in the rest of the ingredients except the edamame and stir thoroughly.
4. Cook for 5 minutes until paste forms and the pepper softens.
5. Once cooked, transfer to a serving bowl and top with some edamame and enjoy!

LOW CARB VEGAN RAMEN

Time: 30 minutes | Serves 1

Kcal 283, Carbs 7g/, Fats 18.9g/, Proteins 16.5g/, Fibers 8g/0.28oz.

INGREDIENTS:

- 15ml/1 tablespoon of olive oil
- 500ml/2 cups of veggies stock
- 34g/2 tablespoons of soy sauce
- 34g/2 tablespoons of tamari
- 34g/2 tablespoons of coconut aminos
- 1 clove of minced garlic
- A pinch of grated ginger
- 1 package of shirataki noodles
- ¼ a block of fried or baked tofu
- A handful of sprouts
- A handful of baby spinach
- 32g/¼ a cup of mixed mushrooms
- Chili flakes
- Seaweed flakes
- Sesame seeds
- Chopped scallions

PREPARATION:

1. On a pan quickly sauté the mushrooms and tofu.
2. Put some oil on a saucepan and add some ginger and garlic to cook on medium heat.
3. Stir for 1 minute or until they get nice and fragrant.
4. Put in some soy sauce and broth and let it simmer.
5. Clean, drain, and rinse the noodles before adding it to the broth and allow the mixture to simmer for 5-10 minutes.
6. Remove the noodles from the broth and place on a serving bowl.
7. Top with some sautéed tofu, mushroom and baby spinach before pouring the broth on the toppings.
8. Garnish and enjoy!

SNACKS

LOW-CARB ZUCCHINI NACHO CHIPS

Time: 25 minutes | Serves 4

Kcal 145, Carbs 2g/0.06oz., Fats 14g/0.49oz., Proteins 1g/0.03oz., Fiber 1g/0.0goz.

INGREDIENTS:

- A pinch of salt
- 375ml/1½ cups of coconut oil
- 15ml/1 tablespoon of Tex-Mex seasoning
- Large zucchini

PREPARATION:

1. Using a Mandolin, chop the zucchini into round thin slices.
2. Put the slices in a colander and season with lots of salt and allow to settle for 5 minutes before squeezing out all the water.
3. Bring the oil up to 180°C/350°F in a skillet and fry the zucchini pieces in the hot oil.
4. Put in a paper towel to get rid of excess oil
5. Add some taco seasoning and there you go!

ALMOND AND SEED MIX

Time: 15 minutes | Serves 10

Kcal 234, Carbs 3g/0.1oz., Fats 21g/0.74oz., Proteins 9g/0.3oz., Fiber 3g/0.1oz.

INGREDIENTS:

- 🍽 30ml/2 tablespoons of olive oil
- 🍽 115g/4 oz. of pumpkin seeds
- 🍽 140g/5 oz. of almonds
- 🍽 115g/4 oz. of sunflower seeds
- 🍽 17g/1 tablespoon of chili paste
- 🍽 A pinch of salt
- 🍽 17g/ 1 tablespoon of ground cumin

PREPARATION:

1. Bring the oil to heat on a large frying pan before adding chili first.
2. Then add almond and the seeds and stir well.
3. Add some salt before sautéing for a few minutes. Remember the seeds and almonds are quite heat sensitive.
4. Allow to cool and put in a glass jar or can.
5. Enjoy as a snack or as a flavor enhancer on salads.

EASY KETO CEREAL

Time: 30 minutes | Served 6

Kcal 207, Carbs 3g/0.1oz., Fats 18g/0.63oz., Proteins 6g/0.2oz., Fiber 1g/0.03oz.

INGREDIENTS:

- 4g/1 teaspoon of ground cinnamon
- 34g/2 tablespoons of sunflower seeds
- 128g/1 cup of almond flour
- A pinch of salt
- 5ml/1 teaspoon vanilla extract
- 30ml/2 tablespoons of water
- 17g/1 tablespoon golden flax meal
- 1½ L/ 6 cups of unsweetened almond milk
- 15ml/1 tablespoon of coconut oil

PREPARATION:

1. Bring the oven to 175°C/350°F.
2. Mix and blend the sunflower seeds, almond flour, cinnamon, flax meal, and salt in a food processor.
3. Pulse while adding in coconut oil and water slowly until you achieve an even dough.
4. On a parchment paper, place the dough and flatten. Cover with another parchment paper before rolling to a 1.5 - 3 mm thickness.
5. Cut into 2.5cm/1 inch squares on a cutting board. Remember to remove the top parchment paper before cutting.
6. With the bottom parchment paper still intact, place in a baking sheet and allow to cook in the oven for 10-15 minutes till the edges are brown.
7. Set aside to cool before separating the pieces.
8. Serve and enjoy

THE 28-DAY KETO VEGAN CHALLENGE

Introduction

A Keto diet is not only good for overall health benefits but also one of the most comfortable diets you can have. In light of this, being vegan is no excuse for not jumping into this bandwagon and enjoying the benefits. For this reason, we have come up with a 28-week challenge to prove that you don't need to be an all carnivore to start a Keto diet plan.

DAY 1

Breakfast: Low carb vegan pancakes

Time: | Serves 2

Kcal 260, Carbs 5.1g/0.18oz., Fats 20.8g/0.73oz., Proteins 9.8g/0.35oz., Fiber 8.8g/0.31oz.

INGREDIENTS:

- 30ml/2 tablespoons of unsweetened almond butter
- 17g/1 tablespoon of ground flax
- 125g/½ a cup of unsweetened almond milk
- 17g/1 tablespoon of coconut flour
- 2g/½ a teaspoon baking powder
- A pinch of salt if you don't use almond butter
- 30ml/2 tablespoons of olive oil

PREPARATION:

1. Lightly put some olive oil on a pan over low to medium heat
2. Mix almond butter and almond milk in a bowl
3. Combine and mix well all the dry ingredients till well blended.
4. Now mix all the wet and dry ingredients until thoroughly blended. Put aside for 5 minutes and let the coconut flour and flux absorb the liquid.
5. Scoop some batter and spread on the pan and cook for 2-5 minutes, flipping the other side when one side is cooked.
6. Top with some almond butter before serving and enjoy!

Lunch: Avocado and radish salad and fennel carrot (See page 35)

Dinner: Pesto zucchini noodles with cherry tomatoes (See page 50)

DAY 2

Breakfast: Carrot cakes pancakes (See page 23)

Lunch: Vegan Keto Tikka Masala

Time: 35 minutes | Serves 5

Kcal 248, Carbs 8.9g/, Fats 21.2g/, Proteins 4.7g/, Fiber 5.6g/

INGREDIENTS:

- 64g/½ a cup of coconut cream
- ½ diced onions
- 2g/½ a teaspoon of cayenne pepper
- 640 g/ 1.4 lb. florets of cauliflower
- 4g/1 teaspoon of ground cumin
- A pinch of salt
- 60ml/4 tablespoons of virgin coconut oil
- 2 cloves of minced garlic
- 17g/1 tablespoon of garam masala
- 4g/1 teaspoon of garam masala

- 2g/½ a teaspoon of cayenne pepper
- 360 g/ 12.7 oz. of crushed tomatoes
- 6 g/ 0.2 oz. of minced ginger
- A pinch of salt
- 15ml/1 tablespoon of olive oil
- 6g/1½ teaspoons of ground paprika
- 120 ml/½ a cup of water
- 32g/1/4 a cup of minced cilantro
- 4g/1 teaspoon of ground cumin

PREPARATION:

1. Bring the oven to a temperature of 220 °C/ 425 °F.
2. Combine the cauliflower florets, salt, and spices in a large bowl before arranging in a baking sheet lined with aluminum foil.
3. Cook for 30 minutes in the oven till tender.
4. Prepare the sauce when the cauliflower is left with 15 minutes.
5. Using a deep skillet, bring the virgin coconut oil to heat before putting in garlic, onion, and ginger and cook for 5 minutes.
6. Put in the spices and cook till nice and fragrant.
7. Add in the tomatoes, water, and coconut cream the stir. Let it simmer for 10 minutes till thick.
8. Put in the cooked cauliflower and some cilantro before stirring.
9. Serve and enjoy while warm!

Dinner: Vegan cauliflower pizza bites (See page 51)

DAY 3

Breakfast: Cheezy Chorizo & Red Pepper Frittata (See page 25)

Lunch: Keto falafels (See page 37)

Dinner: HARISSA PORTOBELLO MUSHROOM

Time: 30 minutes | Serves 4

Kcal 405, Carbs 20g/0.71oz., Fats 34g/1.2oz., Proteins 10g/0.35oz., Fiber 14g/0.5oz.

INGREDIENTS:

Portobello mushrooms

- 🍽 4g/1 teaspoon onion powder
- 🍽 6 collard green leaves
- 🍽 45ml/3 tablespoons of divided olive oil
- 🍽 450g/1 lb. of Portobello mushrooms
- 🍽 4g/1 teaspoon of ground cumin
- 🍽 60g/1/4 a cup of spicy harissa

Guacamole

- 🍽 2 medium avocados
- 🍽 Pinch of salt
- 🍽 17g/1 tablespoon of chopped cilantro
- 🍽 30ml/2 tablespoons of lemon juice
- 🍽 34g/ 2 tablespoons of chopped tomatoes
- 🍽 34g/2 tablespoons of chopped red onions

PREPARATION:

10. Detach the stem from the mushroom, rinse and dry

11. Combine and mix, harissa, cumin, onion powder, and half of the olive oil in a bowl.

12. Brush the mushrooms with the harissa marinade before allowing them to marinate preferably for 15 minutes.

13. Clean, halve and pit the avocados before scooping into a bowl.

14. Mash the avocados before mixing with chopped tomatoes, cilantro, some salt, lemon juice, and red onions.

15. Gently wash the collard greens before removing the tough stems and setting it aside.

16. After marinating, heat the remainder of the olive oil in a sauté pan and throw in the mushrooms.

17. Sauté the mushrooms on medium heat and cook for 6 minutes tossing frequently until they turn brown.

18. Let the mushrooms sit for 2 minutes before slicing

19. Serve by filling a collard leaf with a few Portobello mushrooms, guacamole, and cilantro.

DAY 4

Breakfast: Keto overnight oats

Time: 5 minutes | Serves 2

Kcal, Carbs, Fats, Proteins, Fiber

INGREDIENTS:

- 🍽 A pinch of Himalayan ground rock salt
- 🍽 3ml/½ a teaspoon of vanilla extract
- 🍽 17g/1 tablespoon of chia seeds

- 🍽 30ml/2 tablespoons of confectioners erythritol
- 🍽 160ml/⅔ a cup of full-fat coconut milk
- 🍽 75g/½ cup of a Hemp heart
- 🍽 5 raspberries

PREPARATION:

1. Add all the ingredients except the raspberries in a container with a lid and mix thoroughly.
2. Allow setting in the refrigerator for at least 8 hours preferably overnight.
3. Put in additional coconut milk till you achieve the desired consistency.
4. Serve in two bowls and serve with some raspberries toppings.

Lunch: Vegan tempeh pumpkin bowl with herb dressing (See page 39)

Dinner: Instant pot pilaf (See page 53)

DAY 5

Breakfast: Oven-baked rutabaga wedges (See page 27)

Lunch: Vegan Keto Bibimbap

Time: 25 minutes | Serves 1

Kcal 247, Carbs 9g/0.32, Fats 13g/0.46oz., Proteins 18g/0.63oz., Fiber 8.7g/0.31oz.

INGREDIENTS:

- 130g/1 cup of cooked cauliflower rice
- 65g/½ a cup of cooked broccoli
- 100g/3.5oz. of baked air-fried tofu
- 4g/1 teaspoon of sesame seeds
- Chopped scallions
- 15ml/ 1 tablespoon of low carb gochujang
- 20g/1/8 of a cup of cooked shiitake mushroom

PREPARATION:

1. Reheat the cauliflower rice and broccoli and bake slightly the tofu.
2. Combine all the veggies and tofu in a bowl, add in some gochujang before garnishing with some sesame seeds and scallion toppings.

Dinner: The Keto vegan Kathmandu curry (See page 56)

DAY 6

Breakfast: Vegan Kebab Rolls with garlic sauce (See page 28)

Lunch: Vegan kale and spinach soup (See page 43)

Dinner: Vegan Keto Walnut Chili

Time: 40 minutes | Serves 5

Kcal 353, carbs 18g/0.63oz., Fats 28g/0.98oz., Proteins 13g/0.45oz., Fiber 8g/0.28oz.

INGREDIENTS:

- 30ml/ 2 tablespoons of extra virgin olive oil
- 2 cloves of minced garlic
- 5 stalks of chopped celery
- 8g/2 teaspoons of chili powder
- 6g/1½ teaspoons of ground cinnamon
- 16g/4 teaspoons of ground cumin
- 2 large minced peppers chipotle in adobo
- 2 diced zucchinis
- 2 diced green bell peppers
- 230g/8 oz. of minced cremini mushrooms
- 420/15 oz. can of diced tomatoes
- 25g/1½ tablespoons of tomato paste
- 750ml/3 cups of water
- 320g/2½ cups of crumbles soy meat
- 8ml/½ a cup of coconut milk
- 128g/1 cup of minced raw walnuts
- 4g/1 teaspoon of unsweetened cocoa powder.

- 🍽 Pepper and salt
- 🍽 34g/2 tablespoons of fresh cilantro leaves
- 🍽 1 sliced avocado
- 🍽 34g/2 tablespoons of sliced radishes

PREPARATION:

1. Bring oil to heat on a large pot over low to medium heat.
2. First, put in the celery and cook for 4 minutes.
3. Add the cinnamon, chili powder, cumin, garlic, and paprika. Mix thoroughly and cook for an additional 2 minutes until they get fragrant
4. Put in the zucchini, bell peppers, and mushrooms and cook for another 5 minutes.
5. Add the chipotle, tomatoes, tomato paste, water, soy meat, coconut milk, cocoa powder, and walnuts.
6. Reduce the heat and let everything simmer for 25 minutes.
7. Add some pepper and salt then top with the sliced avocados, radishes, and some cilantro.

DAY 7

Breakfast: Peanut butter chia pudding

Time: 3 hrs. 10 minutes | Serves 8

Kcal 232, Carbs 6.4g/0.22oz., Fats 19g/0.67oz., Protein 8.5g/0.3oz., Fiber 3.8g/0.13oz.

INGREDIENTS:

- 🍴 128g/1 cup of plain peanut butter
- 🍴 30g/¼ a cup of chia seeds
- 🍴 160g/1¼ cup of unsweetened almond milk
- 🍴 15ml/1 teaspoon of vanilla essence
- 🍴 60ml/¼ a cup of unsweetened maple syrup
- 🍴 2g/½ a teaspoon of crushed peanut
- 🍴 Drops of monk fruit extract

PREPARATION:

1. Put every ingredient in the blender
2. Blend for 1 minute stopping midway to scrape the bottom to attain a smooth creamy consistency.
3. At this stage check the for sweetness and add more maple syrup or drops monk fruit extract if not as sweet as you want it to be.
4. Pour into 8 jars, having 80ml of ⅓ per jar
5. Refrigerate for 3 hours to get that creamy texture and flavor.
6. Serve with crushed peanut butter toppings.

Lunch: Vegan Buddha bowl (See page 41)

Dinner: Air fryer crispy tofu (See page 54)

DAY 8

Breakfast: Vegan tofu scramble (See page 30)

Lunch: Keto Tabbouleh salad

Time: 25 minutes | Serves 4

Kcal 149, Carbs 5g/0.17oz., Fats 14g/0.49oz., Proteins 2g/0.07oz., Fiber 2g/0.07oz.

INGREDIENTS:

- 64g/½ cup of raw cauliflower rice
- 3 cloves of chopped garlic
- 1 diced and seeded tomato
- 4 thinly sliced scallions
- 40g/⅓ cup of chopped mint
- 30ml/2 tablespoons of lemon juice
- 190g/1 ½ cups of chopped parsley
- 60ml/¼ cup of olive oil
- A pinch of salt
- A pinch of ground pepper

PREPARATION:

1. Mix and combine every ingredient thoroughly in a bowl
2. Put aside for the flavors to blend.
3. Serve and enjoy!

Dinner: Air fryer crispy tofu (See page 54)

DAY 9

Breakfast: Low carb eggplant towers (See page 31)

Lunch: Zucchini Walnut salad (See page 45)

Dinner: The zucchini Lasagna

Time: 1 hr. 20 minutes | Serves 9 squares

Kcal 395, Carbs 19g/0.67oz., Fats 35.9g/1.27oz., Proteins 6.8g/0.25oz., Fiber 6.7g/0.23oz.

INGREDIENTS:

- 380g/3 cups of macadamia nuts
- 8g/2 teaspoons of dried oregano
- 64g/½ a cup of chopped fresh basil
- 30ml/2 tablespoons of lemon juice
- A pinch of black pepper
- A pinch of salt
- 15ml/1 tablespoon of extra virgin oil
- 250ml/1 cup of water
- 32g/1/4 a cup of vegan parmesan cheese
- 3 medium zucchini squashes
- Jar of marinara sauce
- 34g/2 tablespoons of nutritional yeast

PREPARATION:

1. Bring the oven up to 180°C/350°F

2. Blend the macadamia nuts in a food processor to a fine composition.

3. Add in fresh basil, nutritional yeast, olive oil, oregano, lemon juice, salt, pepper, water, and parmesan cheese.

4. At this point taste and add seasoning accordingly.

5. Line the zucchini slices in the marinara sauce in a dish.

6. Coat the zucchini slices with the ricotta mixture. Top with some more marinara sauce and place another layer of zucchini slices.

7. Continue spreading and stacking until you exhaust all products. Just remember that the last two layers should be zucchini then the sauce. Top off with the parmesan cheese before covering with a foil.

8. Cook in the oven for 45 minutes then remove the foil before baking for another 15 minutes.

9. Allow cooling before serving with some fresh basil on the side.

DAY 10

Breakfast: Vegan Keto bagels

Time: 50 minutes | Serves 6

Kcal 209, Carbs 2g/0.07oz., Fats16.4g/0.58oz., Proteins 4.4g/0.16, Fiber 7.4g/0.26oz.

INGREDIENTS:

- 112g/4 oz. tahini
- 4g/1 teaspoon baking powder
- 56g/½ a cup of flax seeds
- A pinch of salt
- Sesame seeds
- 250ml/1 cup of water
- 20g/1/4 a cup of psyllium husks

PREPARATION:

1. Bring the even up to 180°C/350°F
2. Combine psyllium husk, baking powder, ground flax seeds, and salt in a bowl then whisk thoroughly.
3. Pour some water to the tahini before mixing till even.
4. Combine the wet ingredients with the dry and mix carefully to achieve a uniform dough.
5. Using your hand, create patties and from circular holes on the patties before laying them on the baking sheet.
6. Top with some sesame seeds before baking for 40 minutes till nice and golden brown.
7. Half, and toast before serving.

Lunch: Vegan butter chicken (See page 47)

Dinner: Peanut red curry noodle bowl (See page 58)

DAY 11

Breakfast: Low carb vegan vanilla protein shake (See page 33)

Lunch: *TRIPLE GREEN KALE SALAD*

Time: 15 minutes | Serves 4

Kcal 135, Carbs 8g/0.28oz., Fats 10g/0.35oz., Proteins 3g/0.11oz., fiber 3g/0.11oz.

INGREDIENTS 1

- 🍽 280g/8 oz. laciniate kale
- 🍽 10ml/2 teaspoons of extra virgin oil
- 🍽 10ml/2 teaspoons of sesame seeds oil
- 🍽 2 cloves of crushed garlic
- 🍽 A pinch of sea salt

INGREDIENT 2

- 🍽 17g/ 1 teaspoon of grated ginger
- 🍽 2 teaspoons of coconut aminos
- 🍽 1 sliced and ripe avocado
- 🍽 A handful of chopped scallions
- 🍽 Orange zest
- 🍽 A handful of chopped snow peas
- 🍽 Hemp seeds

PREPARATION:

1. Wash and rinse the kales before pat drying
2. Remove the stem and stack 5 leaves of kale before rolling and slicing to smaller pieces
3. Thoroughly mix the chopped kales with ingredients 1 and massage in using your hands.
4. Add the second ingredients, mix well and serve.

Dinner: Low carb vegan ramen (See page 60)

DAY 12

Breakfast: Carrot cake pancakes (See page 23)

Lunch: Vegan butter chicken (See page 47)

Dinner: Spicy Red Curry Roasted Cauliflower Soup

Time: 40 minutes | Serves 6

Kcal 224, Carbs 14g/0.49oz., Fats 18g/0.63oz., Proteins 4g/0.14oz., Fiber 4g/0.14oz.

INGREDIENTS:

- 🍽️ 15ml/1 tablespoon of olive oil

- 🍽️ A single large cauliflower

- 🍽️ 1 medium diced yellow onion

- 🍽️ 1L/ 4 cups of vegetable broth

- 🍽️ 68g/4 tablespoons of Thai red curry paste

- 🍽️ 400g/14 oz. of unsweetened coconut milk

- 🍽️ Green onions diced

- 🍽️ 15ml/1 tablespoon of lemon juice

- 🍽️ A pinch of Himalayan pink salt

PREPARATION:

1. Bring the oven to 175°C/350°F.
2. Slice the onion into quarters and the cauliflowers into florets. Sprinkle some olive oil before laying them on a tray with parchment paper and bake for 20 minutes.
3. Add the vegetable broth, bakes cauliflower, and onions to a blender and blend till smooth.
4. Empty the puree into a pot then add red curry paste, salt, lemon juice, and coconut milk then heat till warm.
5. Serve with green onion toppings

DAY 13

Breakfast: Cinnamon roll muffins

Time: 20 minutes | serves 20 muffins

Kcal 112, Carbs 3g/0.12oz., Fats 9g/0.32oz., Proteins 5g/0.18oz., Fiber 2g/0.07oz.

INGREDIENTS:

- 64g/½ a cup of almond flour
- 34g/2 scoops of vanilla protein powder
- 4g/1 teaspoon of baking powder
- 64g/½ a cup of almond butter
- 17g/1 tablespoon of cinnamon
- 125ml/½ a cup of pumpkin puree
- 125ml/½ a cup of coconut oil
- 10ml/ 2 teaspoons of lemon juice
- 17g/1 tablespoon of granulated sweetener of choice
- 32g/1/4 cup of coconut butter
- 60ml/1/4 cup of almond milk

PREPARATION:

1. Bring the oven to 175°C/350°F then use a muffin tin tray, line with parchment paper.

2. Combine and mix well all the dry ingredients before mixing with the wet ingredients.

3. Distribute the batter on each liner before cooking till nice, soft, and risen for 15 minutes.

4. Allow cooling for 5 minutes.

5. Prepare the glaze by combining the almond milk, coconut butter, lemon juice, and the sweetener before mixing till even.

6. Pour on the muffin tops and let it firm.

Lunch: Keto falafels (See page 37)

Dinner: Peanut red curry noodle bowl (See page 58)

DAY 14

Breakfast: Cheezy Chorizo & Red Pepper Frittata (See page 25)

Lunch: Mushed cauliflower with garlic and avocado

Time: 20 minutes | Serves 4

Kcal, Carbs 10.9g/0.38oz., Fats 13.1g/0.46oz., Proteins 4.1g/0.44oz., Fiber 4.2g/0.43oz.

INGREDIENTS:

- 1 sliced avocado
- Pepper
- Salt
- 15ml/1 tablespoon of olive oil
- 2 cloves of minced garlic

PREPARATION:

1. Chop the cauliflower into small pieces (florets) before rinsing
2. Steam the florets for 5 minutes.
3. Put some oil in a pan, heat, and add in some garlic then cook for 30 seconds till nice and fragrant.
4. Now drain the water from the steamed cauliflower and add in the garlic and any other optional spice.
5. Mash the cauliflower and serve with avocado seasoned with olive oil, pepper, and salt.

Dinner: Vegan cauliflower pizza bites (See page 51)

DAY 15

Breakfast: Vegan Tofu scramble (See page 30)

Lunch: Zucchini and walnut salad (See page 45)

Dinner: Balsamic Roasted Brussel sprouts

Time: | Serves 6

Kcal 199, Carbs 11g/0.39oz., Fats 15g/0.54oz., Proteins 7g/0.25oz., Fiber 4g/0.14oz.

INGREDIENTS:

- 1 kg trimmed Brussel spouts
- 30ml/2 tablespoons balsamic vinegar
- 60ml/1/4 a cup of olive oil
- A pinch of sea salt
- 4g/1 teaspoon of black pepper

PREPARATION:

1. Bring the oven up to 180°C/350°F
2. Mix up the Brussel sprouts, balsamic vinegar, and olive oil in a bowl and massage evenly.
3. Move the coated Brussel sprouts to a baking dish and add some pepper and seas salt.
4. Bake in the oven for 20 minutes then remove, toss around and bake for another 20 minutes till nice and brown.
5. Serve while hot

DAY 16

Breakfast: Keto Granola

Time: 25 minutes | Serves 8

Kcal 277, Carbs 3g/0.11oz., Fats 25g/0.88oz., Proteins 7g/0.25oz., Fiber 5g/0.18oz.

INGREDIENTS:

- 192g/1½ cups of roughly chopped mixed nut
- 128g/1 cup of unsweetened shredded coconut
- 64g/½ a cup of blanched almond flour
- 80ml/1/3 a cup of Keto maple syrup

PREPARATION:

1. Bring the even up to 180°C/350°F then line the oven with parchment paper.
2. Mix all the ingredients in a deep bowl making sure everything blends well.
3. Spread the mixture evenly on a tray.
4. Cook for 25 minutes till the edges become brown.
5. Allow cooling before breaking into manageable pieces.

Lunch: Low carb eggplant towers (See page 31)

Dinner: Pesto Zucchini Noodles with Cherry Tomatoes (See page 50)

DAY 17

Breakfast: Vegan Kebab rolls with garlic sauce (See page 28)

Lunch: Zucchini Cauliflower Fritters

Time: 10 minutes | 8 burgers

Kcal 255, Carbs 2g/0.07oz, Fats 7g/0.25oz., Proteins 4g/0.14oz., Fibers 3g/0.1oz.

INGREDIENTS:

- 🍴 1g/1/4 teaspoon black pepper
- 🍴 2g/½ teaspoon salt
- 🍴 32g/1/4 a cup of all-purpose gluten-free flour
- 🍴 ½ a head of chopped cauliflower

PREPARATION:

1. Using a food processor grate the zucchini
2. Steam the zucchini before and blend in a food processor.
3. Use a thin kitchen towel to squeeze and drain all the water.
4. Mix up everything in a bigger bowl into a nice dough and shape into patties using your hand.
5. Fry on the pan using coconut oil over medium heat. Remember to flip on one side is ready.

Dinner: The Keto vegan Kathmandu (See page 56)

DAY 18

Breakfast: Low carb vegan vanilla protein shake (See page 33)

Lunch: Vegan kale and spinach soup (See page 43)

Dinner: Pan-Seared Tandoori Tofu

Time: | Serves

Kcal, Carbs 2.9g/0.1oz., Fats 5.6g/0.19oz., Proteins 5.8g/0.2oz., Fiber 1g/0.03oz.

INGREDIENTS:

- 🍴 4g/1 teaspoon of black pepper
- 🍴 A block of extra firm tofu
- 🍴 17g/1 tablespoon of red pepper flakes
- 🍴 17g/1 tablespoon of paprika
- 🍴 17g/1 tablespoon of sea salt
- 🍴 30ml/2 tablespoons of olive oil
- 🍴 17g/1 tablespoon of cumin
- 🍴 17g/1 tablespoon cayenne pepper
- 🍴 17g/1 tablespoon of Turmeric

PREPARATION:

1. Spread olive oil on a large pan and put over low to medium heat
2. Combine all the spices in a separate bowl.
3. Dip the tofu slices in the spice before frying cut phase-down for 2-3 minutes before flipping to the other side to cook as well.
4. Serve after cooling

DAY 19

Breakfast: Keto Peanut Butter Smoothie

Time: 1 minute | Serves 1

Kcal 198, Carbs 8g/0.28oz., Fats 17g/0.6oz, Proteins 6g/0.21oz., Fiber 6g/0.21oz.

INGREDIENTS:

- 🍽 17g/1 tablespoon of peanut butter
- 🍽 1 serving liquid stevia
- 🍽 125ml/½ a cup of almond milk
- 🍽 17g/1 tablespoon of cocoa powder

- 🍽 34g/2 tablespoons of powdered peanut butter
- 🍽 ¼ medium avocado
- 🍽 ¼ cup of ice

PREPARATION:

1. Blend all the ingredients except ice in a food processor to a consistent composition.

2. You can add milk if it is too thick. Add extra peanut butter powder if it's too thin.

3. Serve with some ice and enjoy

Lunch: Vegan Buddha bowl (See page 41)

Dinner: Instant pot pilaf (See page 53)

DAY 20

Breakfast: Oven-baked rutabaga wedges (See page 27)

Lunch: *Vegan Mushroom Burgers*

Time: 40 minutes | Serves 3

Kcal 171, Carbs 3.5g/0.12oz., Fats12g/0.42oz., Proteins12g/0.42oz., Fiber 3.3g/0.12oz.

INGREDIENTS:

- A pinch of sea salt

- A pinch of cracked black pepper

- 17g/1 tablespoon chia seeds

- 32g/¼ of a cup tahini

- 51g/3 tablespoons protein powder

- 1g¼ a teaspoon of dried ground rosemary

- 225g/8 oz. mushrooms

PREPARATION:

1. Bring the oven up to 180°C/350°F before lining with baking sheet and parchment paper

2. Cook the mushrooms in a larger skillet and over medium heat till soft

3. Let cool, drain excess water and coarsely chop the mushrooms by hand or using a food processor

4. Put in the tahini, chia seed, rosemary, salt, and pepper before stirring everything up.

5. Let the mixture stay for some time for the chia seeds to absorb in moisture and mixture gets thick enough

6. Add in the protein powder a scoop at a time till enough.

7. Create 3 equal patties by hand and bake in the oven for 20-25 minutes flipping it halfway through

8. Allow cooling, and enjoy.

Dinner: Vegan cauliflower pizza bites (See page 51)

DAY 21

Breakfast: Low carb vanilla protein shake (See page 33)

Lunch: Zucchini and walnut salad (See page 45)

Dinner: Korma Curry Sauce

Time: 20 minutes | Serves 4

Kcal 82, Carbs 5g/0.17oz., Fats 8g/0.28oz., Proteins 1g/0.03oz, Fiber 1g/0.03oz

INGREDIENTS:

- 1 avocado
- 15ml/1 tablespoon of coconut oil
- Thumb sized fresh ginger
- Roughly chopped medium onion
- 3 cloves of chopped garlic
- 8g/2 teaspoons of curry powder
- 10ml/2 tablespoons of tomato puree
- A pinch of salt
- 51g/ 2 tablespoons of ground almonds
- 400ml tin of coconut milk

PREPARATION:

1. Peel, pit, and scoop the avocados into a bowl before adding some salt and pepper to taste.

2. Bring the coconut oil to heat on a medium size pan.

3. Put in onion, ginger chili and garlic then cook for 2 minutes till soft

4. Add in the curry powder and salt then stir further for 2 minutes

5. Pour in the almond milk, tomato puree, and almonds then let simmer for a while.

6. Put the mixture in a blender to thicken and get that nice creamy composition.

7. Fry some onions in a pan and add in veggies of your choice.

8. Put in some more coconut milk and let simmer for 3 minutes till nice and soft.

9. Serve with some seasoned avocado on the side and naan bread.

DAY 22

Breakfast: Keto Vegan chocolate waffles

Time:20 minutes | Serves 4 waffles

Kcal 224, Carbs 3.8g/0.13oz., Fats 17.5g/0.62oz., Proteins 5.5g/0.19oz., Fiber 10.5g/0.37oz.

INGREDIENTS:

- 56g/½ a cup of coconut flour
- 51g/3 tablespoons of granulated sweetener
- 30g/3 tablespoons of cocoa powder
- 2g/½ a teaspoon of baking powder
- 10g/2 teaspoons of psyllium husks
- A pinch of salt
- 56g/¼ cup of softened coconut oil
- 250ml/1 cup of non-dairy milk

PREPARATION:

1. Preheat your waffle iron according to instructions
2. Mix and whisk together the dry ingredients in a mixing bowl
3. Add coconut oil to the dry ingredients and mix till you achieve a tough dough
4. Add in the milk progressively as you stir till you achieve the desired consistency
5. Allow the mixture to sit for 3 minutes to set
6. Make four equal portions from the dough and make the waffles according to the manufacturer's instructions
7. Remove from the iron, allow cooling before serving.

Lunch: Vegan Buddha Bowl (See page 41)

Dinner: Peanut Red Curry Noodle Bowl (See page 58)

DAY 23

Breakfast: Carrot cake pancakes (See page 23)

Lunch: Broccoli salad with fresh dill

Time 10 minutes | Serves 4

Kcal 413, Carbs 5g/0.17oz.., Fats 42g/1.48oz.., Protein 4g/0.14oz.., Fiber 3g/0.1oz.

INGREDIENTS:

- Salt and ground black pepper
- 128g/1 cup vegan mayo
- 453g/ 1lb. broccoli
- 96g/ ¾ cup fresh dill

PREPARATION:

1. Reduce the broccoli to small florets and chop the stalks into small pieces.
2. Introduce the florets and stalk pieces into salted boiling water for 5 minutes.
3. Drain and add the other ingredients and stir.
4. Season with pepper to your liking

Dinner: Air Fryer crispy tofu (See page 54)

DAY 24

Breakfast: Vegan tofu scramble (See page 30)

Lunch: Peanut Red Curry Noodle Bowl (See page 58)

Dinner: Vegan Keto Pasta Alfredo

Time: 25 minutes | Serves 4

Kcal 340, Carbs 5g/0.18oz.., Fats 5g/0.18oz.., Protein 7g/0.3oz.., Fiber 3g/0.1oz..

INGREDIENTS:

- 🍽 Cauliflower rice

- 🍽 4 cloves of minced garlic

- 🍽 15ml/2 teaspoons of olive oil

- 🍽 375ml/1 ½ of unsweetened almond milk

- 🍽 51g/3 tablespoons of nutritional yeast

- 🍽 190g/1 ½ cups of soaked cashew

- 🍽 15ml/1 tablespoon of lemon juice

- 🍽 Minced parsley

- 🍽 Salt and pepper

- 🍽 1 bag Mann's Kohlrabi Linguine

PREPARATION:

1. Briefly microwave the cauliflower rice
2. Add garlic to a pan and sauté over medium to low heat until golden brown
3. Once done, blend it together with cauliflower rice, cashews, almond milk, lemon juice, and the nutritional yeast
4. Blend till smooth before adding some salt and pepper
5. Sauté the bag Mann's Kohlrabi Linguine for about 7 minutes before adding the sauce and mix well.
6. Serve in 4 plates then top with some parsley.

DAY 25

Breakfast: Blueberry smoothie

Time: 5 minutes | Serves 1

Kcal 415, Carbs 10g/0.35oz.., Fats 10g/0.35oz.., Proteins 4g/0.14oz.., Fiber 1g/0.03oz.

Ingredient

- 🍽 205ml/ 7 oz. coconut milk
- 🍽 8ml/½ tablespoon of lemon juice
- 🍽 32g/¼ cup of blueberries
- 🍽 1g/¼ teaspoon of vanilla extract

PREPARATION:

1. Carefully blend all the ingredients to achieve a smooth texture.

Lunch: Vegan butter chicken (See page 47)

Dinner: Low carb vegan ramen (See page 60)

DAY 26

Breakfast: Vegan kebab rolls with garlic sauce (See page 28)

Lunch: Broccoli salad with fresh dill

Time 10 minutes | Serves 4

Kcal 413, Carbs 5g/0.17oz.., Fats 42g/1.48oz.., Protein 4g/0.14oz.., Fiber 3g/0.1oz.

INGREDIENTS:

- Salt and ground black pepper
- 128g/1 cup vegan mayo
- 453g/ 1lb. broccoli
- 96g/ ¾ cup fresh dill

PREPARATION:

1. Reduce the broccoli to small florets and chop the stalks into small pieces.
2. Introduce the florets and stalk pieces into salted boiling water for 5 minutes.
3. Drain and add the other ingredients and stir.
4. Season with pepper to your liking

Dinner: The Keto Vegan Kathmandu curry (See page 56)

DAY 27

Breakfast: Low carb eggplant towers (See page 31)

Lunch: Vegan tempeh pumpkin bowl with herb dressing (See page 39)

Dinner: Avocado and radish salad with fennel and carrots

Time 45 minutes | Serves 2

Kcal, Carbs 18g/0.63oz., Proteins 15g/0.53oz., Fats 43g/1.5oz., Fiber 18g/0.63oz.

INGREDIENTS:

- An avocado
- 1 bulb fresh fennel
- Ground black pepper
- 2 carrots
- 30ml/ 2 tablespoons of olive oil
- 57g/ 2 oz. of leafy greens
- 57g/ 2 oz. of sesame seeds
- 75ml/5 tablespoons of tamari soy sauce
- 170g/6 oz. of radishes

PREPARATION:

1. Bring the oven to a temperature of 180°C/350°F then line with a baking sheet with parchment paper.
2. Put sesame seeds in the sauce to marinate for about 15 minutes
3. Bake the marinated seeds for 6-10 minutes. Remember sesame seeds.
4. Peel, pit and dice the avocado into a bowl then combine with chopped carrots, radishes, and fennel.
5. Add some leafy green toppings before seasoning with pepper and generous amounts of olive oil.
6. Serve with baked sesame seeds.

DAY 28

Breakfast: Chocolate avocado smoothie

Time: 10 minutes | Serves 1

Kcal 268, Carbs 6g/0.21oz., Fats 18.5g/0.65oz., Proteins 7.7g/0.27oz., fiber 12g/0.42oz

INGREDIENTS:

- ½ an avocado
- 17g/1 teaspoon of hemp powder
- 45ml/3 tablespoons of erythritol
- ⅔ cup of ice cubes
- 250ml/1 cup of unsweetened vanilla almond milk
- 25g/1½ tablespoon of unsweetened cocoa powder

PREPARATION:

1. Put everything in a blender and mix thoroughly at full speed for 1 minute.
2. Taste and add more drops of erythritol if needed. You could also add the ice cubes to make your smoothie thicker.
3. Finally, blend to desire thickness then serve.

Lunch: Zucchini and walnut salad (See page 45)

Dinner: Pesto Zucchini Noodles with Cherry Tomatoes (See page 50)

Printed in Great Britain
by Amazon